BRINGING CHRIST TO THE CRISIS

Kevin Tarver
Bringing Christ To The Crisis

—

Published by - Spines
ISBN: 979-8-89569-160-1

BRINGING CHRIST TO THE CRISIS

Finding Faith, Forgiveness, and Justice Amidst Tragedy

Kevin Tarver

CONTENTS

INTRODUCTION

Powerful Promise:

"In Bringing Christ to the Crisis, you will discover the transformative power of faith in the face of unimaginable pain, the strength to forgive those who seem unforgivable, and the courage to fight for justice with unwavering resolve. This book will guide you on a journey from despair to hope, offering spiritual tools and profound insights to navigate your own crises and emerge stronger, more compassionate, and deeply connected to God's purpose in your life."

The Intersection of Faith and Life:

From the very beginning, my life was steeped in faith. I was raised in a home where the presence of God was not just acknowledged but revered, a home where the foundations of our lives were built on the solid rock of scripture and prayer. My father, a steadfast pastor, guided our family with a deep conviction in the power of the Holy Spirit. My mother, though quiet in her demeanor, wielded an unwavering faith that moved mountains and touched the very heart of God with her prayers.

In our household, faith wasn't just something we practiced on

Sundays—it was the very air we breathed. Sometimes if the doors of the church were open seven days a week, and more often than not, my siblings and I found ourselves there, rather it was church service, bible study, prayer night, choir rehearsal or a revival we where there, sometimes three or four times on a Sunday. Under the watchful eyes of our parents and the strict teachings of our Pentecostal church, we were nurtured in an environment where the miraculous was not only possible but expected.

I grew up witnessing the extraordinary: the sick healed, the lame walking, demons cast out, and lives transformed by the sheer power of God's presence. These were not just stories from ancient texts but living, breathing realities that unfolded before our eyes. We were taught to walk by faith and not by sight, to trust in God's promises even when the world around us seemed to crumble. Our lives were a testament to the truth that with God, nothing is impossible.

This foundation of faith was more than a set of beliefs—it was a way of life that shaped everything I would become. It taught me resilience in the face of adversity, hope in the darkest of times, and the assurance that no matter what life might throw at me, God's hand was always at work. Little did I know that this deep-rooted faith, cultivated in the sanctuaries of my childhood, would one day be the anchor that held me steady when my world was shattered.

When Faith Faces the Unthinkable

In the stillness of a cold, unforgiving night, my world shattered. The phone call that no parent ever wants to receive brought the unthinkable into my reality: my son, my precious child, was gone—taken from this world by an act of police brutality so senseless and cruel that it defied comprehension. In that moment, I was plunged into a darkness that seemed impenetrable, where every breath was a struggle, and every prayer felt like a cry into the void.

How could this happen? Why did God allow this? These questions reverberated through my mind, unanswered, as the weight of grief threatened to crush my spirit. I was faced with a crisis that challenged not only my heart but also the very foundation of my faith. Yet, it was in the midst of this overwhelming pain that I began to experience Christ in a way I never had before—not as a distant figure, but as a constant presence guiding me through the storm.

This book is a testament to that journey—a journey of faith tested by fire, of grief that sought justice as well a ongoing fight, and of a spirit that refused to be broken. It is a story of bringing Christ to the crisis, not by finding easy answers, but by walking a path of faith, forgiveness, and fortitude in the face of unimaginable loss.

As you read these pages, I invite you to walk with me through the

"

valleys of despair and onto the mountains of hope, to witness the power of faith in the darkest of times, and to find solace in the promise that Christ is with us, even in the most harrowing moments of our lives. My prayer is that this story will not only bring comfort to those who are grieving but also inspire a relentless pursuit of justice, anchored in the love and righteousness of Christ.

For in the end, it is not the crisis that defines us, but how we bring Christ into it—how we allow His light to shine through our darkest hours, and how we turn our pain into a powerful force for good. This is my story, but it is also the story of countless others who have faced the unthinkable and found that even in the deepest sorrow, there is a divine purpose that can lead us toward healing and hope.

We all have our storm mine was police brutality, yours may be a natural disaster, rape, sex trafficking, domestic violence, abuse, political violence, gun violence there are so many ways disaster and tragedy comes and we grieve our losses. It's good to know that no matter what our experience may be , nothing can separate you from the love of God.

Romans 8:37-39

[37]No, in all these things we are more than conquerors through him who loved us. [38]For I am convinced that neither death nor life, neither angels nor demons, neither the present nor the future, nor any powers, [39]neither height nor depth, nor anything else in all creation, will be able to separate us from the love of God that is in Christ Jesus our Lord.

THE FOUNDATION OF FAITH

Being raised in such a strict Pentecostal environment taught me to see the world through a spiritual lens. I learned that there was more to life than what met the eye, that behind every situation and every struggle, there was a spiritual reality at work. The Holiness church emphasized living a life set apart, not conforming to the patterns of the world, but instead being transformed by the renewing of the mind. This shaped my worldview in profound ways.

I understood from a young age that the battles we face in life are not just physical or emotional—they are spiritual. We were taught to walk by faith and not by sight, to trust in God's promises even when circumstances seemed impossible. This faith gave me a resilience that would carry me through many challenges, a hope that would sustain me in the darkest of times.

The Holiness tradition emphasized the importance of personal holiness and purity, teaching us to live in a way that reflected the character of Christ. It was about more than just avoiding sin; it was about actively pursuing a life that glorified God in every aspect. This pursuit of holiness shaped not only my personal conduct but also my understanding of justice, compassion, and the inherent dignity of every human being.

As I grew older, this spiritual foundation became the anchor of my life. It shaped the way I interacted with the world, how I responded to adversity, and how I understood my purpose. It taught me that my life was not my own, but a vessel through which God could work. Little did I know that this deeply rooted faith, nurtured in the sanctuaries of my childhood, would one day be the strength I would need to face unimaginable loss and to fight for justice in a world that often seems so far from God's will.

Growing up, the foundation of faith that my parents laid for me was unshakeable, but as I stepped out into the world beyond our church walls, I began to see cracks in the surface of the life I had known. The early signs of crisis were subtle at first, but they grew more glaring with each passing year. I began to see the world for what it was—a place where injustice, racism, and the abuse of power were all too common, especially for people who looked like me.

Racism was not just a distant concept or something we read about in history books—it was a reality that we lived with every day. I saw it in the way people looked at us, in the way opportunities were denied, and in the unspoken rules we had to follow just to stay safe. My oldest brother was one of the first to feel the sting of this reality when he and his friends lost their scholarships, not because of anything they had done, but because of the color of their skin. The police, abusing their power, made sure that their futures were taken away, and with it, the hopes and dreams that my family had worked so hard to build.

I saw the devastation that drugs brought to our community, how they tore families apart and destroyed lives. It wasn't just something that happened in far-off places—it was happening right in front of me. Friends I had grown up with, people who had once been full of potential and promise, were now shadows of their former selves, trapped in the cycle of addiction. It was a crisis that seemed to consume everything in its path, and no one was immune from its reach.

We learned quickly that we couldn't live our lives like everyone else. We had to be constantly aware of how we acted, how we responded, and where we went. There were areas we knew to avoid, places where being caught after dark could mean trouble, or worse. Our lives were governed by an unspoken code, a survival strategy that was passed down from one generation to the next. Be in before dark. Don't draw attention to yourself. Always show respect, even when it isn't shown to you. These were the rules we lived by, rules that were born out of necessity in a world that was far from just.

These early signs of crisis were a stark contrast to the life of faith and hope that I had known in church. They were reminders that while our faith could sustain us, it couldn't shield us completely from the harsh realities of the world. I began to see that our walk by faith was not just about trusting in God's promises—it was also about navigating a world that often seemed to be against us, a world where the forces of darkness were all too real.

As these crises unfolded around me, they began to shape my understanding of the world. I saw that our faith was not just a refuge, but a call to action, a call to stand against the injustices we faced. It was a realization that would grow stronger in the years to come, as the challenges became more personal, more painful, and ultimately, more life-changing.

THE CRISIS UNFOLDS
THE INCIDENT

January 21, 2020, is a day that forever changed my life, a day that began like any other but ended in unimaginable pain. My son, Darius, was in the midst of a mental health crisis—an event that should have called for care, compassion, and de-escalation. Instead, it ended in tragedy at the hands of those sworn to protect him. Darius was a 23-year-old young man, highly respected, a student at the University of North Texas, on the dean's list, and on the cusp of achieving his second degree in Criminal Justice. He was an active member of the National Organization of Black Law Enforcement and was passionate about making a difference in the world. But on that day, all of that was ripped away.

It began a week earlier when Darius was in a near-fatal car accident. He was unresponsive when help arrived, and we rushed to the hospital, praying and bringing Christ to the crisis. He was admitted to ICU Trauma, and while he was heavily sedated, we were told he was going to be fine. The hospital discharged him much sooner than I could imagine, the next mourning after church I was getting ready to go back and visit my son I called down to the hospital and his mother told me he was already being released, and despite my concerns and unease of being released less than 24 hours straight from ICU Trauma, they sent him home with his mother. Over the following days, Darius showed signs of distress I was unaware of until afterwards, but none of us could have anticipated the events that would follow.

On the day before Martin Luther King Jr. Day, Darius attended three different church services, ultimately dedicating and surrendering his life to Christ at the third one Shiloh Baptist Church. The message preached that morning was "You Have To Have Your Own Testimony", which my son heard the call and it moved him. The pastor was about to close out but the spirit of God wouldn't allow him, so he got back up and said God said one more person needs to surrender their life, my son got up and went down to the alter and surrendered to God. I would have never imagined that less than 24 hours later, he would be gone. Early on the morning of January 21st, Darius was in crisis again. His roommate and others called 911 because he was knocking out hallway lights with a frying pan crying out to God not trying to hurt anyone. When the Denton police arrived, instead of finding a way to help him as he kept crying out to God repeatingly saying my heavenly father, the enemy took it as a threat they escalated the situation. As he descended the stairs, pointing to the sky and crying out to God, the officers tased him and then shot him rendered no aid or tried to arrest or restrain him let him back up and shot him 2 more times, despite the fact that he posed no imminent threat or danger. His last words were, 'My heavenly Father, I will not fear.' But in those moments, my worst fear had become reality.

The Immediate Aftermath

The news of Darius's death shattered my world. The emotions that flooded me were overwhelming—why, how, not me. It was a helpless feeling, knowing that there was nothing I could have done to protect him in that moment. Tears flowed constantly, my heart heavy with the weight of loss and the chaos that followed. Anger surged within me, anger at the injustice of it all, anger at the police who had failed to see my son as the person he was—a young man in need of help, not harm. There was blame, grief, and a profound sense of being alone. The reality of his death was almost too much to bear, tearing apart the fabric of our family, leaving a void that could never be filled.

As a man, a father, a protector, I felt utterly powerless. How could this happen to my son, a young man who had dedicated his life to serving others? I had never imagined burying one of my children, and yet here I was, facing the unimaginable. In the midst of my grief, I turned to the words of Psalm 55, where the psalmist cries out to God in desperation: 'My heart is sore pained within me: and the terrors of death are fallen upon me. Fearfulness and trembling are come upon me, and horror hath overwhelmed me. And I said, Oh that I had wings like a dove! for then would I fly away, and be at rest.'

In those moments, I had to bring Christ into the crisis, just as I had always done. It was the hardest thing I'd ever had to do, because this time, the crisis was my own. I cried out to God, asking why, questioning how He could allow something like this to happen when I had been serving Him faithfully, both as a pastor and as a police chaplain. My son was about to enter law enforcement himself, to be part of the change we so desperately needed, but now that hope was gone. The pain was unbearable, the sorrow endless, but I knew I had to lean on Christ, even when it seemed like the hardest thing I'd ever done.

You feel overwhelmed, unable to sleep or find rest. Tears come at unpredictable moments, and you begin to wonder how God could allow such suffering. But in those darkest moments, my heart cried out to the Lord. I had moments of anger, knowing that this should never have happened. Everything felt chaotic, as if the ground had been ripped out from under me. But then, amid the chaos, I realized something profound —God had chosen me, not because I was so strong or great, but because He could use me, even in my pain, for His glory.

It wasn't easy to see it at first, but God began to reveal that through this tragedy, He had a purpose for me. People saw strength in me when I felt nothing but struggle. They saw boldness when all I felt was fear. Like Job, who endured immense suffering because God trusted him, I began to understand that my pain had a purpose. This tragedy wasn't just about loss; it was about leading me to a new calling, one that would bring justice and change, not just for my son, but for so many others.

Learning to bring Christ into the crisis has been the fight of my life. I've been to the White House, met with national leaders, and fought for changes in laws and policies, all because my pain has led me to my purpose. Darius's life was sacrificed for the kingdom, and through DJTJUSTICENETWORK.ORG, his legacy will live on. We will fight for justice, bring change, and continue to bring Christ to the crisis, ensuring that his death was not in vain.

Wrestling with God
The Struggle Within

In the quiet moments of solitude, we often find ourselves in the midst of a spiritual struggle, one that echoes the ancient story of Jacob. In Genesis 32:22-29, Jacob wrestled with a mysterious figure throughout the night, refusing to let go until he was blessed. This powerful story speaks to the very core of our own battles—times when we grapple with God, seeking answers, clarity, and peace in the midst of life's storms.

Just as Jacob found himself alone in the night, wrestling with an unknown man, we too can find ourselves in the dark, grappling with questions that seem to have no answers. The spiritual battles we face are real, and they often leave us feeling isolated, overwhelmed, and at odds with the very faith that once seemed unshakable.

The Wrestling Match

The journey of faith is not always a smooth path. There are times when we must confront the harsh realities of life, where the darkness seems to close in, and we are left with nothing but our pain, our doubts, and our questions. This is the wrestling match with God—a time when we are forced to confront our deepest fears and our most profound doubts.

In my own life, this struggle became all too real in the aftermath of my son's death. The tragedy that unfolded left me questioning everything I had ever believed. I found myself screaming at God, demanding answers, and struggling to find any sense of peace or understanding. The spiritual practices that once brought me comfort—prayer, scripture reading, meditation—felt distant and almost impossible to engage with. It was as if I was wrestling with God Himself, refusing to let go until I received some semblance of a blessing, some reason for the suffering.

THE PRESENCE OF EVIL

We live in a world where the battle between good and evil is ever-present. Corruption, violence, injustice, and hatred seem to surround us at every turn. The news is filled with stories of shootings, genocide, civil wars, and the rise of false prophets. The persecution of believers continues to increase, and it often feels as though evil is winning the day. Yet, despite all of this, we hold onto the belief that God is still God, that His goodness will ultimately triumph over the forces of darkness.

The Bible tells us to overcome evil with good, but when we are in the midst of our own personal crises, it can be hard to see that truth. The pain, the anger, the overwhelming sense of loss can cloud our vision and make it difficult to trust in God's plan. I know this all too well. In those moments of deepest despair, it's natural to question God, to cry out in frustration, and to feel as though you are fighting a losing battle.

UNDERSTANDING GOD'S PLAN

But as I've walked this difficult path, I've come to realize that God has a plan for each of us, even when we cannot see it. Our journeys are filled with twists and turns that we would never choose for ourselves, yet each step is leading us toward the purpose that God has set before us. The road is not easy, and the process of understanding it can be painful. But God's program is one of growth, transformation, and ultimate victory.

Yet, we must also be aware that there is another force at work—Satan, the enemy of our souls, who seeks to oppose and resist God's people and His purpose. Satan's kingdom is real, and his agents are actively working against the plans of God. This is a spiritual warfare, and we cannot afford to be deceived. We must stand strong in our faith, knowing that God is our refuge and our fortress.

Standing on the Promises

In times of crisis, when the world seems to be falling apart around us, we must stand on the promises of God. Psalm 91 reminds us of the protection and refuge that God provides for those who trust in Him:

"He that dwelleth in the secret place of the most High shall abide under the shadow of the Almighty. I will say of the Lord, He is my refuge and my fortress: my God; in him will I trust..."

These words are not just comforting; they are a call to arms in the spiritual battle we face. When the terror by night and the arrows that fly by day seem overwhelming, we are reminded that God's truth is our shield and buckler. We do not need to fear, for God has given His angels charge over us, to keep us in all our ways.

Wrestling for Understanding

The story of Jacob and the struggle he faced with God is a powerful reminder that we too must wrestle with our faith, especially in the face of tragedy. We must be willing to confront our doubts, our fears, and even our anger toward God. But just as Jacob did not let go until he was blessed, we too must hold on, even when it feels like the night will never end.

God's blessing often comes in ways we do not expect, and it may leave us with a limp—a reminder of the battle we have fought. But it also leaves us transformed, with a deeper understanding of who we are and who God is. Like Jacob, we may come away from the struggle with a new name, a new identity, forged in the fires of suffering and refined by the hands of God.

Faith in the Midst of the Battle

As we wrestle with God, seeking understanding in faith, we must remember that the battle we face is not just against flesh and blood, but against the spiritual forces of evil in the heavenly realms. This is why we must cling to the truth of God's Word, standing firm in our faith, and trusting that God is with us in the midst of the battle.

In the story of Joseph, who was thrown into a pit by his own brothers, we see another example of God's plan at work in the midst of suffering. Joseph's journey was filled with hardship, betrayal, and pain, yet through it all, God was with him, guiding him toward the fulfillment of his destiny. What his brothers meant for evil, God used for good.

This is the hope we hold onto in our own struggles—that even in the darkest moments, God is working for our good, bringing about His purpose in our lives. We may not understand it at the time, and we may even fight against it, but in the end, we will see that God's plan is perfect, and His love for us is unending.

The spiritual struggle is real, and it is one that we all must face at some point in our lives. But as we wrestle with God, seeking understanding and clarity in the midst of our pain, we can take comfort in knowing that He is with us every step of the way. We may come away from the struggle with scars, but those scars are a testament to the strength we have gained and the faith that has been refined.

In the end, we are not alone. Just as Jacob was blessed after his night of wrestling, we too will find our blessing, our peace, and our understanding as we continue to trust in God's unfailing love and sovereign plan. Let us hold on, even when the night is long, and trust that the dawn will bring the blessing we seek.

The Fight for Justice —Turning Grief into Action and Addressing Spiritual Advocacy

A Journey I Never Expected

When I used to see the images on TV—grieving mothers, attorneys, protests, and marches—I never imagined I would find myself on the front lines of this battle. The thought of standing where I stand today, having met with Presidents Trump and Biden, working on reform and legislation, was far from my mind. Yet, this journey, birthed from the deepest pain, has led me to places I never thought I'd go. I've stood alongside some of the top civil rights attorneys in the country, national leaders & legislators,spoken on platforms I never dreamed of, and formed partnerships with national organizations dedicated to justice. But this path was not one I chose; it was one that was thrust upon me, one that I walk for my son, Darius.

The Transformation of Grief into Action

After Darius's death, grief engulfed me like a tidal wave, threatening to drown me. It would have been easy to succumb to it, to let it paralyze me. But I knew that if I didn't stand up, if I didn't speak out, then Darius's death would have been in vain. The pain became a catalyst for change, turning my sorrow into a fierce determination to fight for justice—not just for my son, but for all the other sons and daughters who have suffered at the hands of a broken system.

The DJT Justice Network was born from this resolve. It became the voice of Darius, a mechanism for peace, and a modern civil rights movement. Inspired by the non-violent approach of Dr. Martin Luther King Jr., we advocate for ONE STANDARD of justice, where all humans are treated equally, regardless of race, religion, or gender. We work tirelessly to initiate, educate, and activate communities across America and beyond, providing the tools needed to understand issues like Qualified Immunity and offering resources to those affected by police brutality or mental illness.

Spiritual Advocacy: The Battle Beyond the Physical

In this fight, I've come to understand that the battle for justice is not just a physical one; it's deeply spiritual. The Bible teaches us that God is a God of justice. Isaiah 30:18 tells us, "For the Lord is a God of justice; blessed are all those who wait for him." And in Psalm 33:4-6, we're reminded that "The Lord loves righteousness and justice; the earth is full of his unfailing love."

This spiritual advocacy is about more than just prayer; it's about embodying the principles of justice that God stands for. It's about standing firm in the belief that, as Exodus 15:3 says, "The Lord is a warrior; the Lord is his name." We must be warriors in this fight, not with violence, but with unwavering commitment to justice. God calls us to be advocates, to fight for those who cannot fight for themselves, and to bring His light into the darkest places.

Building a Legacy of Change

Through the DJT Justice Network, Darius's legacy lives on. We're not just fighting for justice in his name; we're building a movement. We're advocating for the creation of centers that are neither hospitals nor jails, where people experiencing mental crises can receive treatment instead of being arrested or killed. We're striving to bring people together, to tell their stories, and to work towards solutions that bring real, lasting change.

The core of our efforts is to bring true justice, accountability, and reform to an unjust culture that has plagued America for far too long. We stand with other families affected by police brutality, knowing that our collective voices are stronger than any one of us alone. Together, we fight for legislative changes that will balance the scales of justice, so that one day, all people can live without fear of those sworn to protect them. However, we must also address those we elect to represent us that also deny recomendations by law enforcement leaders who do stand and support change and more accountability but hands are tied, because police union power and money.

A Call to Action

This chapter of my life of Darius's legacy, is a call to action. It's a call to everyone who reads these words to stand with us, to lend your support, and to become part of this fight for justice. The Bible says in Isaiah 42:13, "The Lord will march out like a champion, like a warrior he will stir up his zeal; with a shout he will raise the battle cry and will triumph over his enemies." We, too, must raise our voices, march out with the same zeal, and triumph over the injustice that seeks to destroy us.

The fight for justice is not easy, and it's not quick. But it's a fight worth fighting. For Darius, for every victim of police violence, and for the future of this country, we must keep pushing forward, turning our grief into action and our faith into advocacy. Together, we can make the difference that our world so desperately needs.

The Power of Advocacy

Advocacy is a powerful tool in the fight for justice. It allows us to raise our voices, to speak truth to power, and to demand change. But advocacy is not just about making noise; it's about creating a sustained effort to bring about real, lasting change. This requires a deep commitment to the cause, a willingness to face opposition, and an unwavering belief in the righteousness of the fight.

Through DJT JUSTICE NETWORK, we have worked to bring attention to the systemic issues that led to Darius's death and to advocate for reforms that can prevent such tragedies from happening to others. This work has involved lobbying for policy changes, organizing community events, and building coalitions with other organizations that share our mission.

Advocacy also means standing in solidarity with those who are suffering, offering support, and letting them know they are not alone. It's about building a community of allies who are committed to fighting for justice together. This work is not easy, but it is essential if we are to create a more just and equitable society.

The Struggle for Justice

The fight for justice is not a sprint; it is a marathon. It requires persistence, resilience, and a deep well of inner strength. There will be setbacks, disappointments, and moments of despair, but we must press on, knowing that the struggle is worth it.

In the fight for justice, we must be prepared to face opposition from those who benefit from the status quo. We must be ready to confront systems of power that are deeply entrenched and resistant to change. But we must also remember that we are not alone in this fight. There are countless others who are standing with us, who share our vision for a more just world.

The road to justice is long and often difficult, but it is a road that we must travel if we are to honor the memory of those we have lost. We fight not just for ourselves, but for the generations to come, so that they may live in a world that is fair, just, and equitable.

Faith in the Fight

As a person of faith, I have found strength in the belief that justice is not just a human endeavor, but a divine mandate. The Bible is filled with calls for justice, with reminders that God is on the side of the oppressed and that He will not tolerate injustice forever. This belief has sustained me in the darkest moments of the fight, reminding me that I am not alone and that the fight for justice is ultimately a part of God's plan.

Psalm 82:3-4 says, "Defend the weak and the fatherless; uphold the cause of the poor and the oppressed. Rescue the weak and the needy; deliver them from the hand of the wicked." These words have been a guiding light for me, reminding me that the fight for justice is not just about seeking retribution, but about upholding the dignity and worth of every human being.

In this fight, prayer has been a source of strength and guidance. When the road has seemed too difficult to bear, I have turned to God for the courage and wisdom to keep going. And in those moments when the fight has seemed hopeless, I have found comfort in knowing that God is ultimately in control, and that His justice will prevail.

MOVING FORWARD WITH PURPOSE

Turning grief into action is not about forgetting the pain or moving on from the loss. It's about finding a way to honor that pain, to give it meaning, and to use it as a force for good in the world. It's about recognizing that our grief can be a powerful tool for change if we allow it to be.

As I continue to walk this path, I do so with the knowledge that the fight for justice is far from over. There is still much work to be done, and I am committed to seeing it through. My son's life was taken from him, but his legacy lives on in the work that we are doing, in the lives that are being touched, and in the changes that are being made.

The fight for justice is a sacred calling, one that requires us to turn our grief into action, our pain into purpose. It is a fight that demands our full commitment, our unwavering determination, and our deepest compassion. As we continue to push forward, let us do so with the knowledge that we are not alone, that our efforts are making a difference, and that justice will ultimately prevail.

In memory of Darius, and for all those who have been wronged, we will continue to fight. We will continue to stand up, to speak out, and to demand justice. And we will do so with the firm belief that love, justice, and truth will ultimately win the day.

The Power of Forgiveness - The Journey to Forgiveness

Forgiveness is perhaps one of the most challenging paths a human heart can walk. As a Christian, a pastor, and a true believer, I have often preached about the importance of forgiveness, but when it came to the men who murdered my son, forgiveness became a heavy cross to bear. They acted as judge, jury, and executioners, delivering a death sentence to my child and leaving me with a life sentence of grief and pain. And yet, the call to forgive still echoes in my soul.

Wrestling with Forgiveness

Mark 11:25 reminds us, "And whenever you stand praying, forgive, if you have anything against anyone, so that your Father also who is in heaven may forgive you your trespasses." But what do you do when the very act of forgiveness feels like a betrayal of your own heart? How do you forgive those who have shown no remorse, who have taken what is most precious to you, and who have left a void that can never be filled?

Forgiveness does not mean forgetting, excusing, or absolving the wrong done. It means finding a way to release the grip of anger and bitterness that threatens to consume you. For almost two years after my son's murder, I was in a dark place. The anger I felt was overwhelming, and there were moments when I contemplated taking justice into my own hands. I felt as though God was distant, that He was not hearing or feeling the depth of my pain.

But God, in His infinite mercy, began to work on my heart. He reminded me of His promises, even when I was in the midst of my despair. Matthew 6:14-15 teaches us, "For if you forgive others their trespasses, your heavenly Father will also forgive you, but if you do not forgive others their trespasses, neither will your Father forgive your trespasses." This was a hard truth to swallow, but it was one I could not ignore.

THE DARK NIGHT OF THE SOUL

In the darkness of those years, I often felt like I was sitting in a hospital waiting room, powerless and without control. Waiting for justice in this David against Goliath battle felt like an eternity, and the weight of it all nearly broke me. I cried out to God, questioning His presence, His love, and His justice. I wondered if He could truly understand the agony of a parent who has lost a child to such brutal violence.

But God is faithful, even when we are not. Isaiah 40:31 tells us, "But those who wait on the Lord shall renew their strength. They shall mount up with wings like eagles, they shall run and not be weary, they shall walk and not faint." As I waited, as I wrestled with God, He began to renew my strength. He reminded me that waiting on Him is not passive; it is an active, intentional reliance on His timing and His will.

THE PROPHETIC WORD

God did not leave me without comfort. He spoke to me through His Word, bringing Isaiah 40:3-5 to my heart:

A voice of one calling: "In the wilderness prepare the way for the Lord; make straight in the desert a highway for our God. Every valley shall be raised up, every mountain and hill made low; the rough ground shall become level, the rugged places a plain. And the glory of the Lord will be revealed, and all people will see it together. For the mouth of the Lord has spoken."

These words reminded me that God was still at work, even in the midst of my pain. He was preparing the way, leveling the mountains of injustice, and revealing His glory in ways I could not yet see.

When I questioned, "Why me?" God answered with Isaiah 41:8-16, assuring me that He had chosen me, that He was with me, and that He would uphold me with His righteous right hand. He promised to turn my pain into a weapon of righteousness, to use me as a tool to thresh the mountains of injustice, and to bring forth His justice in His time.

THE JOURNEY CONTINUES

Forgiveness is not a one-time event; it is a journey, a process that requires continual surrender to God. It is a daily decision to lay down the anger, the desire for revenge, and the bitterness that can so easily take root in our hearts. Psalm 27:14 encourages us, "Wait on the Lord; be of good courage, and He shall strengthen your heart; wait, I say, on the Lord!"

As I continue this journey, I hold on to the promises of God. I trust that He will bring justice in His way and in His time. I choose to forgive, not because it is easy, but because it is necessary for my own healing and for the fulfillment of God's purposes in my life.

Forgiveness does not mean I forget what happened to my son, nor does it mean that I excuse the actions of those responsible. It means that I release them into God's hands, trusting that He will deal with them according to His perfect justice. It means that I refuse to allow the anger to consume me, to dictate my actions, or to steal my peace.

This is the journey of forgiveness—one that I walk with God, trusting in His strength, His justice, and His love. It is a journey that I will continue to walk, day by day, as I seek to honor my son's memory and fulfill the calling that God has placed on my life.

Rebuilding and Healing

The Potter and the Clay: A Journey Through Brokenness

In the aftermath of unimaginable loss, I found myself in a place of complete brokenness. It's a feeling that's hard to describe unless you've lived it—a deep, hollow void where faith once stood firm. I used to hear sermons about the potter and the clay, about how God molds us through our trials. But it wasn't until my own heart was shattered that I truly began to understand what it means to be remolded by God.

For almost two years, I was lost, merely going through the motions. The fire in my spirit had dimmed, and the God I once felt so close to seemed distant and unresponsive. It was as if the very ground beneath me had crumbled, and I was left grasping for something, anything, to hold on to. My loving wife saw it too. She came to me, her words cutting through the fog of my despair, telling me she didn't even recognize me anymore. It was a wake-up call that shook me to my core. I was on the brink of walking away from everything—my faith, my calling, my very identity.

Feeling Alone in the Fight

As I tried to navigate this dark valley, it seemed like the world moved on without me. Friends, family, even spiritual leaders who had once stood by my side seemed to disappear. I saw so many pastors at vigils, standing tall and making grand speeches about justice and support. But when it came time to fight, to truly stand in the trenches, they were nowhere to be found. I hosted Monday night calls with other families who had also lost loved ones to police brutality. We shared our pain, our struggles, our hopes. I invited pastors to join, to offer some comfort, some guidance. But when I asked these families who had been their biggest support, not a single one mentioned a pastor.

It was a sobering realization. The people who were supposed to shepherd us through the darkest times were often absent. It's not that they didn't care—they prayed, they offered words of encouragement. But prayer alone wasn't enough. We needed action. We needed someone to walk with us, to fight with us. In the end, I found more solace and strength in the company of those who had walked this road themselves than in the words of those who hadn't.

HEALING THROUGH SURRENDER

Psalm 34:18 says, "The LORD is close to the brokenhearted and saves those who are crushed in spirit." But in my darkest moments, I felt anything but close to God. It took time—time and a deliberate decision to cast my cares upon Him. I had to let go, to stop trying to carry the weight of my grief and anger alone. You don't live on this planet long without trouble, but the question is: Do you really give it to God?

I learned that true healing comes not from avoiding the storm, but from finding God in the midst of it. Each trouble is an opportunity for God to do amazing things, to show His power in ways we never imagined. Instead of praying for the outcome I wanted, I began to pray for God's presence. And in that presence, I found strength. There's nothing too hard for God. In our storm, He is calling us to purpose and providing all we need to fulfill it.

REBUILDING WITH PURPOSE

As I began to rebuild, I realized that God wasn't just restoring me to who I was before—He was making me into something new. 2 Peter 1:3-4 tells us that God has given us everything we need for life and godliness. He's given us His precious promises, and through them, we become partakers of His divine nature.

This journey of healing isn't just about me, it's about the purpose God has placed before me. It's about using the pain, the loss, the grief, to drive me forward in the fight for justice to be a voice for those who can no longer speak for themselves. It's about building something out of the ashes, something that can stand as a testament to God's faithfulness, even in the darkest times.

SEEKING TRUE RELATIONSHIP

In this process, I've had to ask myself: Am I seeking a relationship with God, or just what I can get from Him? Philippians 4:6-7 says, "Do not be anxious about anything, but in every situation, by prayer and petition, with thanksgiving, present your requests to God. And the peace of God, which transcends all understanding, will guard your hearts and your minds in Christ Jesus."

It's easy to approach God with a list of demands, expecting Him to fix everything. But real healing, real peace, comes from seeking Him for who He is, not just for what He can do. It's about trusting Him with the outcome, whatever it may be and finding peace in His presence, knowing that He is with us every step of the way.

In the end, rebuilding and healing is not a destination; it's a journey. It's a process of daily surrender, of trusting God with our broken pieces and allowing Him to create something beautiful out of our pain. And as we walk this path, we find that He is closer than we ever imagined, binding up our wounds, and giving us the strength to keep moving forward.

BRINGING CHRIST TO THE CRISIS - "FAITH IN ACTION"
TURNING PAIN INTO PURPOSE

In life we all face challenges, tragedies, and struggles that can leave us broken and questioning our faith. When my son was taken from me, I was plunged into a darkness I never imagined. The pain was so deep, so consuming, that it felt like there was no way out. But as I've walked this path, I've come to realize that pain, when surrendered to God, can lead to purpose. My pain has become my passion, and now, that passion drives me to help others heal, just as I am healing.

The journey to healing is not a solitary one. We heal through advocacy, through reaching out to others who are hurting and standing with them in their darkest hours. I never asked to be a leader, but like Jonah, I discovered that you can run, but you can't hide from God's calling. It's in those moments of surrender that we begin to see the bigger picture, the purpose that God has for our lives.

CHANGING YOUR FOCUS

One of the most important lessons I've learned is the power of focus. If you focus on what you lack, on what hurt you or caused your pain, it becomes difficult to hold on to faith in God's provision. Psalm 23:1 says,

"The Lord is my shepherd, I lack nothing." This verse reminds us that God is our provider, that in Him, we have everything we need.

When we face trials, we have a choice: we can run to God, or we can run away from Him. I chose to run to Him, even when it felt like He was distant. I've made it my mission to educate communities, to build programs, and to bring light into the darkness that so many families face. Each story is a battle, and every battle is the story of a person—a father, a mother, a son, or a daughter. These stories must be told, and they must lead to action.

DEFINING AND DEMANDING CHANGE

In this fight for justice, it's not enough to simply protest or voice our frustrations. We must define clear, actionable policies, communicate these policies through the stories of those affected, and work tirelessly to see these policies enacted. Too many battles are fought in isolation, too many movements are hindered by a lack of clarity and direction. But when we come together, when we unite in a common cause, we can achieve real, lasting change.

As I've grown in this journey, I've also sought to educate myself, to become certified in areas that qualify me and legitimize my voice as I speak across the country. We must move away from our carnal way of thinking and begin to think, believe, and fight with a Kingdom mindset.

KINGDOM THINKING

Jesus said in John 17:16, "They are not of the world, even as I am not of the world." As Christians, we are called to be different, to follow Christ's word and reflect it in our actions. Our fight is not just against flesh and blood, but against spiritual forces that seek to destroy and divide. John 18:36 reminds us that Jesus' kingdom is not of this world, and while we are here, we are ambassadors for Christ.

To achieve restoration, we must undergo a process of transformation. First, we must replace our hearts of stone with hearts of flesh, as Ezekiel 36:26 says. God wants to give us new hearts and a new spirit. Second, we must renew our minds, as Romans 12:2 instructs, by focusing on God's word and allowing it to transform our thinking. Third, we must revive our spirits, as Romans 6:4 declares, through the resurrection of Jesus Christ, who gives us new and everlasting life. Finally, we must return to God, as Romans 5:10 tells us, through the saving work of Jesus on the cross.

Preparing for the Kingdom

There is a powerful force gathering—a force more powerful than any army on earth. It is the army of the Lord, preparing the way for His Kingdom. This army is not distinguished by uniforms but by its unwavering faith and commitment to God's will. It is hidden now, but soon enough, every soul on earth will hear its trumpets blow. Where it marches, it will conquer; where it stands, it will not be moved. Hebrews 11:27 speaks of the faith that kept Moses going, even in the face of overwhelming odds. That same faith is what will keep us going as we fight for justice and prepare for the greatest event of all time—the coming of God's Kingdom.

A Message of Hope

To all those facing crisis, I encourage you to stand strong in faith, even in the darkest hour. We are more than conquerors through Christ. Jeremiah 51:20-23 says, "Thou art my battle axe and weapons of war: for with thee will I break in pieces the nations, and with thee will I destroy kingdoms." God has the ability to do great things through us if we yield ourselves to Him and allow Him to work in our lives.

This is not just a fight for justice; it is a fight for the Kingdom of God. We are His battle axes, His weapons of war, and through us, He will bring about change. We must stand together, fight together, and move forward in common cause, with our eyes fixed on the One who is invisible, yet ever-present.

As we prepare for the greatest event of all time, let us remember that God is with us. He is our strength, our shield, and our victory. And as we bring Christ to the crisis, we will see His Kingdom come, His will be done, on earth as it is in heaven.

Conclusion: A New Path Forward

As we reach the end of this journey together, I want to encourage you to embark on your own path with renewed strength, purpose, and faith. Life is filled with moments of pain, loss, and injustice, but it is also brimming with opportunities for healing, growth, and change. My story, like so many others, is one of unimaginable tragedy, but it is also a testament to the power of resilience, the importance of justice, and the unshakeable foundation of faith. I currently yet serve on my home

In times of crisis, it is easy to feel overwhelmed, isolated, and defeated. But remember, you are not alone. There is a community of believers, advocates, and warriors who stand ready to support you, to fight with you, and to pray for you. Lean on them, just as you lean on God. Together, we can stand up against the injustices that plague our world, and together, we can work towards a better future.

Seeking justice is not an easy task, but it is a righteous one. Whether you are battling systemic racism, fighting for the rights of the oppressed, or standing up against any form of injustice, know that your efforts are not in vain. Every act of courage, every word of truth, and every step you take toward justice makes a difference. It may feel like you are up against an insurmountable force, but remember the words of Scripture: "If God is for us, who can be against us?" (Romans 8:31).

As you face your own challenges, I urge you to keep your faith at the forefront of your journey. Faith is not just a belief; it is a powerful force that can move mountains, heal wounds, and bring light into the darkest places. When you feel weak, allow God's strength to carry you. When you are filled with doubt, let His promises remind you of the hope that lies ahead. And when you are faced with the choice between despair and determination, choose to walk in faith, knowing that God is with you every step of the way.

This new path forward is not without its obstacles, but it is paved with purpose. It is a path that calls you to be a voice for the voiceless, a champion for the oppressed, and a beacon of hope in a world that desperately needs it. It is a path that leads to healing, not just for yourself, but for others who are walking through their own valleys of despair.

So, as you move forward, do so with courage. Seek justice, love mercy, and walk humbly with your God (Micah 6:8). Stand firm in your convictions, even when the road is difficult, and never lose sight of the power that lies within you—the power to make a difference, to bring about change, and to be a vessel of God's love and justice in this world.

May your journey be blessed, and may you find peace, strength, and purpose as you continue to walk this new path forward.

Written By Kevin E Tarver Sr.

In Loving Memory of Darius Jerrell Tarver "DJ"

He was a bright light in this world-full of love, passion, and potential. His smile could brighten any room, and his heart for others was undeniable he loved to volunteer and serve.Though his life was needlessly and tragically cut short, by what he was working to become, his spirit continues to inspire and fuel a movement for justice, change, and compassion. Darius will always be remembered for the joy he brought to those around him, and his legacy lives on through the fight for justice in his name, He is forever loved and deeply missed.

"A Fallen Eagle"

You're Forever In Our Hearts
DARIUS JERRELL TARVER
"DJ"
September, 13 1996 - January 21, 2020